Inside the World's most Fun

Paper Company

"The Office"

By Tim Morris

Question 1-20

1. The casting team originally wanted who to audition for the role of Dwight?

2. John Krasinski, Mindy Kaling, and who else were all, at one point, interns at Late Night with Conan O'Brien

3. Who almost didn't work in The Office because he was committed to another NBC show called Come to Papa?

4. During his embarrassing Dundie award presentation, whom is Michael Scott presenting a Dundie award when he sings along to "You Sexy Thing" by '70s British funk band Hot Chocolate?

5. In "The Alliance" episode, Michael is asked by Oscar to donate to his nephew's walkathon for a charity. How much money does Michael donate, not realizing that the donation is per mile and not a flat amount?

6. Which character became Jim's love interest after he moved to the Stamford branch in season three and joined the Scranton office during the merger?

7. What county in Pennsylvania is Dunder Mifflin Scranton branch located?

8. What is the exclusive club that Pam, Oscar, and Toby Flenderson establish in the episode "Branch Wars"?

9. What substance does Jim put office supplies owned by Dwight into?

10. What is the name of the employee who started out as "the temp" in the Dunder Mifflin office?

11. Rainn Wilson did not originally audition for the part of the iconic beet farm-ing Dwight Schrute, instead he auditioned for which part?

12. Dwight owns and runs a farm in his spare time. What does this farm primarily produce?

13. In "Diversity Day" episode what famous comedian's stand-up routine does Michael imitate?

14. In the episode "The Client", the employees were reading Michael's movie script. Which employee read the part of Goldenface?

15. What does Michael burn his foot on?

16. Who are the three main members of the party planning committee?

17. What does Michael pretend to fire Pam over in season one?

18. What kind of sandwich does Michael have a dream about when he's the head of Michael Scott Paper Company?

19. What's the name of Dwight's porcupine who he used to make it look like Jim was pranking him?

20. What's in the thermos that Michael offers Pam during morning deliveries for the Michael Scott Paper Company?

Answers 1-20

1. John Krasinski

2. Angela Kinsey

3. Steve Carell

4. Ryan

5. $25

6. Karen Filippelli

7. Lackawanna County

8. Finer Things Club

9. Jello

10. Ryan

11. Michael Scott

12. Beets

13. Chris Rock

14. Oscar

15. A George Foreman Grill that he was cooking bacon on

16. Phyllis, Angela, and Pam

17. Stealing Post-It notes

18. Peanut butter and tunafish

19. Henrietta

20. Milk and sugar

Questions 21- 40

21. What brand is Michael Scott wearing on the day he accidentally wearing a woman's suit?

22. Who does Michael wear on his head during the activity on diversity day?

23. During the episode, "Prince Family Paper," what's the secret signal that Dwight and Michael agree on using?

24. In the episode, "Diwali", who attempts to kiss Pam?

25. How does Michael describe the wine in the episode, "Dinner Party"?

26. Who was a phone operator for 1-800-Dentist when she auditioned for The Office?

27. Which one of Michael's girlfriends in The Office was played by Steve Carell's real-life wife?

28. Who was responsible for casting The Office characters?

29. In the episode "Basketball," after the game between the office workers and warehouse workers, one of the office workers is shown continuously making shots. Which employee is it?

30. What can Dwight Shrute supposedly raise and lower at his will?

31. Which warehouse employee was engaged to Pam?

32. What movie does Michael say that Dwight cried during?

33. Who calls Jim by the nicknames "Tuna" or "Big Tuna"?

34. At Jim and Pam's wedding in the "Niagara" episode, what was Kevin wearing on his feet?

35. What does Jim use to make Dwight salivate in "Phyllis' Wedding"?

36. What does Michael eat instead of ice cream because they don't have any?

37. In the episode "The Coup", the members of the Stamford branch play what video game with each other?

38. What of the following colors does Angela think is "whore-ish"?

39. Jim Halpert knows the flavor of yogurt that Pam likes best, what is it?

40. Who took over Pam as the receptionist after she went to art school in season 5?

Answers 21- 40

21. MISSsterious

22. Martin Luther King Jr.

23. Licking your lips

24. Michael

25. An oaky afterbirth

26. Angela Kinsey

27. Carol

28. Allison Jones

29. Kevin

30. His cholesterol

31. Roy

32. Armageddon

33. Andy

34. Tissue Boxes

35. Altoids

36. Mayo and black olives

37. Call of Duty

38. Green

39. Mixed Berry

40. Ryan

Questions 41- 60

41. Who runs the warehouse below the Dunder Mifflin offices?

42. What does Dwight keep a pair of in his car for special occasions?

43. What is Toby's daughter's name?

44. What is the name of the actor who plays Toby Flenderson?

45. Which actor shares his entire name with his character?

46. In 2019 Jenna Fischer and who else started an Office re-watch podcast entitled "The Office Ladies"?

47. In the episode "Fun Run", who are the three employees that go out to eat in the middle of the run?

48. Who served on the jury for the Scranton strangler case?

49. Who punches a hole in the wall in between Michael's office and the conference room?

50. NBC passed a pilot for a spin-off called "The Farm." Who was it about?

51. After the show was first picked up, what did NBC planned on retitling the series in order to differentiate it from the original British version?

52. What actor starred in the British version of The Office?

53. Who is the proud owner of a Cornell hockey bobblehead?

54. Throughout the show it was revealed that one of the members of the office graduated High School with Michael. Who was it?

55. In the Season 4 pilot episode "Fun Run", what cause does Michael organize a fun run for?

56. What is the number one rated Country and Western station in Scranton, Pennsylvania? (hint: it's a bumper sticker on Dwight's desk)

57. What color does Dwight paint Michael's office when he thinks he's taking over Michael's job?

58. In what episode does Jim propose to Pam?

59. Which network produced "The Office"?

60. What is the middle name of Gabe Lewis?

Answers 41- 60

41. Darryl

42. Birkenstocks

43. Sasha

44. Paul Lieberstein

45. Creed Bratton

46. Angela Kingsey

47. Creed, Oscar and Stanley

48. Toby Flenderson

49. Andy

50. Dwight Schrute

51. "The American Workplace"

52. Ricky Gervais

53. Andy

54. Phyllis

55. Rabies

56. Froggy 101

57. Black

58. "Weight Loss"

59. NBC

60. Susan

Questions 61- 80

61. What actor played Robert California?

62. Which of Angela's cats does Dwight freeze?

63. Which cast member was having an affair with Angela's fiancé, the senator?

64. Which office employee did Michael hit with his car?

65. Who started the fire?

66. What is Michael's username for the online dating website?

67. What vegetable does Michael force feed Kevin?

68. Whose mother does Michael date?

69. What is Scranton's nickname?

70. In the season 2 episode "Christmas Party," what Secret Santa gift does Jim get Pam?

71. Who convinces Dwight that he is being recruited by the CIA?

72. What is the name of Kevin's cover band?

73. Where does Michael Scott move to start his new life with Holly?

74. Angela, played by Angela Kinsey, mentions that her favorite song is what?

75. In the episode "Basketball," who does Michael say is on the team, 'of course'?

76. Where did Michael get his "World's Best Boss" mug?

77. In the "St. Patrick's Day" episode, who gets sick on their first date with Andy?

78. What did Phyllis ask Michael to do in her wedding?

79. Who wins the Fun Run in season 4?

80. What is the name of Phyllis' husband who also happens to work in the same office complex?

Answers 61- 80

61. James Spader

62. Sprinkles

63. Oscar

64. Meredith

65. Ryan

66. Little Kid Lover

67. Broccoli

68. Pam

69. The Electric City

70. Teapot

71. Pam

72. Scrantonicity

73. Boulder, Colorado

74. Little Drummer Boy

75. Stanley

76. Spencer Gifts

77. Erin

78. Push her father down the aisle in his wheelchair

79. Toby Flenderson

80. Bob Vance

Questions 81-100

81. What song does Michael dance down the aisle to during Pam and Jim's wedding?

82. Who is the Human Resources representative at Dunder Mifflin?

83. In the episode "Andy's Play", Andy Bernard performed in a local theatre production of what?

84. In the episode "Take Your Daughter to Work Day," one employee's daughter is flirting with Ryan Howard. Whose daughter was it?

85. What is the the name of the annual employee awards night on the show?

86. In the episode, "Goodbye Michael," what does Pam say Michael seems full of at the end of the episode?

87. In the episode "Chair Model," Pam would receive Michael's chair when he got a new one. Who would get Pam's chair?

88. After the Fun Run to beat Rabies, to whom is the oversized check made out?

89. Based on where he eats most often, what is Michael Scott's favorite restaurant?

90. What art school did Pam go to?

91. How does Jan break Michael's TV in the "Dinner Party" episode?

92. What actor on The Office shot the opening credit footage?

93. What actor from The Office and John Krasinski went to the same high school?

94. What item of clothing does Michael insist on having dry cleaned?

95. Who is the Regional Manager at Dunder Mifflin?

96. Who wins the bronze medal in the episode, "Office Olympics"?

97. When is Michael's birthday?

98. In almost every meeting, Stanley is seen doing what?

99. Jenna Fischer kept what after the series wrapped up?

100. Who is the Assistant to the Regional Manager?

Answers 81- 100

81. "Forever" by Chris Brown

82. Toby

83. Sweeney Todd

84. Stanley

85. Dundies

86. Hope

87. Creed

88. Science

89. Chili's

90. Pratt Institute

91. With a Dundie award

92. John Krasinski

93. B.J. Novak

94. His jeans

95. Michael Scott

96. Jim

97. March 15

98. A crossword puzzle

99. Pam's engagement ring

100. Dwight Schutte

Questions 101-120

101. Who was sent to anger management?

102. Which character speaks the the first line of the series and which character delivers the final line?

103. Who plays Todd Packer, a former employee and Michael's friend?

104. What is the last name of the individual responsible for diversity day training?

105. What is Erin's first name?

106. Which of the company's founders committed suicide?

107. Which restaurant chain was Pam banned from?

108. During the first dundies episode, which employee received the "Don't go in there after me" award?

109. Who is Michael Scott's favorite actress?

110. During Michael's diversity day training, what race was on Stanley's note card?

111. What is the name of the book that Michael Scott "wrote"?

112. In the first episode, during his prank. what does Michael accuse Pam of stealing?

113. What is printed on Michael's coffee mug?

114. When Michael signs the diversity day form, who's name does he sign?

115. What movie is the office watching on movie Monday when Jan comes to visit?

116. Why doesn't Michael want to do Meridith's intervention on Groundhog Day?

117. Michael claims to be part Native American Indian. How much Indian?

118. How many people get their arms cut off in a baler each year?

119. There is a female warehouse staff member Michael thinks is named pudge. What is her real name?

120. What is the name of the disease that pam invents, where your teeth turn to liquid and drip down the back of your throat?

Answers 101- 120

101. Andy

102. Michael Scott (Steve Carell), Pam Beesly (Jenna Fischer)

103. David Koechner

104. Brown (Mr. Brown)

105. Kelly

106. Robert Mifflin

107. Chili's

108. Kevin

109. Meryl Streep

110. Black

111. Somehow, I Manage

112. Post-it notes

113. World's Best Boss

114. Daffy Duck

115. Varsity Blues

116. He celebrates privately

117. 2/15

118. 10

119. Madge

120. Spontaneous Dento-Hydroplosion

Questions 121-140

121. How many times has Meredith been divorced?

122. Who wears the face mask while playing in the basketball game?

123. What does Jim put for Dwight's middle name on his ID badge?

124. What is Andy's middle name?

125. Michael invited Pam along to the job fair because the school was her alma mater, what was his first reason?

126. How many pounds does Jim offer to lose for the weight loss challenge?

127. Michael asks the office what the number one cause of death is in America. What is Dwight's response?

128. Quote: Bankruptcy is nature's do-over.

129. Quote: There's too many people on this earth. We need a new plague.

130. Daryl taught Michael some black man phrases. Which one is missing? Fleece it out, dinkin flicka, bippity boppity give me the zoppity

131. Quote: Cat heaven is a beautiful place, but you don't get there if you're euthanized.

132. What is the brand of ladies suit that Michael accidentally buys?

133. What is kevins guess, when betting on how many jellybeans are in the container at Pam's desk?

134. Who does Angela name her son after?

135. What is the name of the security guard?

136. Martin Nash spent some time in prison before coming to Scranton, what was he arrested for?

137. Who does Michael attempt to buy drugs from to frame Toby?

138. Who did Michael choose to pick the new health care plan for the branch?

139. Who's car is hit with a watermelon during the safety training episode?

140. What was Jim's plan B for marrying Pam?

Answers 121- 140

121. Twice

122. Dwight

123. Fart

124. Baines

125. Eye candy

126. 65 pounds

127. Shotgun weddings

128. Creed

129. Dwight

130. Goin' Mach Five

131. Angela

132. Missterious

133. 10

134. Her cat

135. Hank

136. Insider trading

137. Vance refrigeration delivery guys

138. Dwight

139. Stanley

140. The church in Niagara Falls

Questions 141-160

141. What does Jim think Michael will say within the first hour of the booze cruise?

142. Quote: I like waking up to the smell of bacon. Sue me. Who said it?

143. What happens to Dwight when he tries to go pick up Michael after burning his foot?

144. What is Michael's cast made of after he burns his foot?

145. Who complains about the men's bathroom being white's only?

146. According to prison Mike, what was the worst thing about prison?

147. How much does Dwight sell the princess unicorn dolls for?

148. Why does Dwight think having all the women in the office at the same time?

149. What does GAI stand for?

150. New York New York, the city so nice they named it twice. What is the other name?

151. At the Michael Scott Paper Company, which corner is "Pam's Corner"?

152. Kevin cuts off the top of the Christmas tree because it is too tall, what does Michael want to do with the top?

153. Jim starts a social club, much like the French Revolution and the Black Panthers. What was it called?

154. What is Michael's favorite flavor of cake?

155. How much does Jim donate to Oscar's Nephew's walk-a-thon?

156. Who's warehouse uniform is Jim wearing while Dwight and Michael are silly stringing the warehouse in Utica?

157. Who has two thumbs and hates Todd Packer?

158. Who is Dwight's Bestish Minch?

159. How many apples does Erin eat while bobbing for apples?

160. Who is the main character in threat level midnight?

Answers 141-160

141. I'm king of the world

142. Michael Scott

143. Crashes into a pole, gets a concussion.

144. Bubble wrap

145. Creed

146. Dementors

Finish the Quote: Dwight might have won the battle, but I will win...the next battle.

147. $200

148. They'll get on the same cycle (wreak havoc on the plumbing)

149. Guys afternoon in

150. Manhattan

151. The one with the copier

152. Sell it to charity

153. The Fist

154. Mint Chocolate Chip

155. $3

156. Madge

157. Jim

158. Michael Scott

159. 2

160. Michael Scarn

Questions 161-180

161. Dwight goes through an extensive selection process to find his assistant to the assistant to the regional manager (this when he finally becomes the manager), who does he choose?

162. Where does Michael go on his international business trip?

163. What is the catchphrase for the princess unicorn doll?

164. When Michael is looking for Jobs after giving Dunder Mifflin his two-week notice, what is the only company he calls for a job?

165. The staff spend an episode debating whether a certain actress is hot. Who is the actress?

166. Dwight doesn't like the Girl Scouts. He thinks it's dangerous to teach young girls what?

167. While Michael is roasting everyone who does he tell, "Your teeth called, your breath stinks?"

168. Michael spends an episode spreading rumors. What is the rumor about Andy?

169. Michael spends an episode spreading rumors. What was dwights?

170. What is andys extension?

171. When Kevin writes a check to Pam for her wedding, what does he write in the memo line?

172. At what event does Erin break up with Gabe?

173. Which president does Gabe believe he bears a resemblance to?

174. There's only one Alfredo's that has good pizza. Which one is it?

175. While Andy is trying to remember the words to the kit Kat bar theme song, what candy does he name?

176. What is the name of the dog that Kevin gets from the fundraiser?

177. Where do Michael and holly move?

178. Who takes over as manager when Michael leaves?

179. What is the name of the volunteer group dedicated to keeping the community safe, of which Dwight is the secretary?

180. What is the name of the lawyer that Michael gets during the sexual harassment episode? Also, the same lawyer he asks Dwight to see if he covers hate crimes.

Answers 161-180

161. Dwight

162. Canada

Finish the Quote: Long Island ice teas areway stronger in Canada.

163. My horn can pierce the sky

164. Prince family paper

165. Hilary Swank

166. Self-esteem and leadership skills

167. Creed

168. That he's gay

169. That he uses store bought manure.

170. 134

171. To loves eternal glory

172. The dundies

173. Abraham Lincoln

174. Alfredo's pizza cafe

175. Snickers bar

176. Ruby

177. Boulder Colorado

178. Deangelo Vickers

179. Knights of the night

180. James P. Albini

Questions 181-200

181. What tv show was Michael on as a child?

182. What tattoo does Andy get on his butt?

183. Which office worker gets invited to Dwight's aunt funeral?

184. How do schrutes make sure that the dead the bury are truly dead?

185. What was Kevin's nickname in high school?

186. What is the name of the game Kevin and Oscar play at their desk that Angela hates?

187. Why does Carol break up with Michael?

187. Putting his face over her ex-husbands on a Christmas card

188. What is the name of Andy's college acapella group?

189. During the office Olympics, who wins flonkertin?

190. What is Bob Vance's profession?

191. What kind of company does creed run out of his car?

192. What is Michael's favorite pizza joint in new york?

193. Who complains about Pam planning her wedding to Roy at the office?

194. What is the first name of the company Jim starts?

195. In which business does Dwight steal the chandelier in his perfect crime?

196. Who is Justice Beaver?

197. What is the name of Ryan's baby?

198. During the first halloween episode Phyllis thinks Dwight is a monk. What was he dressed as?

199. What singing tv show does Andy try out for?

200. What is Michael's online profile name for the dating website?

Answers 181-200

181. Fuddle bundle

182. A nard dog

183. Oscar

184. Shotgun to the face

185. Kool aid man

186. Hate ball

188. Here comes treble

189. Phyllis

190. Refrigeration

192. Fake ID

Sbarro

193. Jim

Finish the quote: I'm like Superman and the people who work here are like the citizens of Gotham City

194. Athlead

195. Tiffany's

196. Crime Fighting Beaver

197. Drake

198. A Sith Lord

199. America's next a Capella sensation

200. Little kid love

Questions 201-220

201. What is Meredith's son profession at the end of the series?

202. What is the name of the band that Phyllis hires for her wedding?

203. When Jim and Pam spend the night at Schutte farms there are several differently themed rooms. Which one were they in?

204. Who was the vallet at Andy's dinner party at Schutte farms?

205. Which employee doesn't have full internet access?

206. What is the name of Michael's men's fancy shoe store idea?

207. What was the flavor of sports drink Michael told Ryan to save while Ryan helped clean Michaels car?

208. What was the group Jim created to anger Dwight during his active manager time?

209. What caused Dwight to put the correct prices on the senators' dog charity auction (what was his reasoning)?

210. What did Dwight put in Michaels hair to remove the gum?

211. Dwight mentioned _____ in the peanut butter used for gum removal and Michaels response was: _____ (multiple words)

212. What did Andy and Kevin have to do to get their Parking spots back during construction?

213. How did Angela know that Dwight mercy killed her cat?

214. What did Michael say to Darryl at the beginning of the Rabies Run check in after he saw Darryl feeding a Squirrel? Darryl says but he's happy! What is Michaels response?

215. What was the neon sign Michael resurrected during the hectic dinner party?

216. What was Michael's reason for dropping the Watermelon baby?

217. What is the main brand of computers in Dunder Mifflin?

218. What operating system do Dunder Mifflin computers use?

219. What does the parachuting poster behind the front desk say?

220. What kind of candy is usually at the front desk?

Answers 201-220

201. Stripper

202. Scrantonicity

203. Irrigation

204. Mose

Finish the quote: I am better than you have ever been or Ever will be

205. Kevin

206. Shoe-la-la

207. Blue Blast

208. The Fist

209. He thought it was a Quaker Auction. You guess the price; you win the prize.

210. Peanut Butter

211. The high Calories and Well just don't leave it on too long.

212. Assemble the Five Families

213. She found the body and a clawed-up bag of French fries in the freezer.

214. He's happy because he's insane!

215. St. Paulis Girl beer sign

216. It was covered in butter. Newborns are slippery.

217. HP, (Gateway, Dell for some)

218. Windows XP

219. Teamwork

220. Jellybeans

Questions 221-240

221. What candy did Jim and Pam bring back from Puerto Rico?

222. How much did Michael pay for the 'Marijuana' to frame Toby?

223. What was the name of the computer assistant Michael made up for the banker who assessed the Scranton branch?

224. What was actually in the Ziploc bag of 'Marijuana' Michael bought?

225. What is the name of Andy's Alma mater?

226. What was Jan's first assistants name?

227. What was Michaels remark after he sipped his wine during charades at the dinner party?

228. How much was the plasma screen TV Jan broke? And how did she break it?

229. What was the character Michael used to scared everyone into thinking prison was bad?

230. What odd type of guards did Prison Mike say were terrible while he was in prison?

231. What did Dwight hide a listening device in so he could eavesdrop on Jim to get Jim fired. A Recording Pen, Jim found the wooden mallard containing Dwight's listening device, what another device did he (Jim) not find?

232. What flavor of sports drink did Michael tell Ryan to put in front cup holder for the purse girls ride home?

233. What song did Michael sulk to in his office when he found out the chair model, he liked was dead?

234. What 'top salesman prize' did Michael buy and try to give the purse saleswoman?

235. At the Employee of the Month ceremony that Dwight rigged, after Jim won, what did the delivery man bring?

236. What was the name of the group of kids that Michael promised college tuition too?

237. What did Michael give in lieu of college tuition to the kids?

238. What did Michael say after getting everyone to quiet down upon telling them he was giving them laptop battery's instead of college tuition?

239. What was the jingle Scott's Tots sang?

240. What was the name of Michael's screenplay?

Answers 221-240

221. Cocoa Leche

222. $500

223. Computron

224. Caprizzi Salad

225. Cornell

226. Hunter

227. That has an oak-ey after birth

228. 200-dollar plasma screen TV, she threw a Dundee at it. Only $1.99/month

229. Prison Mike

230. The Dementors. A Wooden Mallard

231. Arctic Chill

232. Goodbye my Lover - James Blunt

233. Koi Pond

234. Starbucks Coffee set

235. A custom cake

236. Scott's Tots

237. Laptop battery's

238. They're lithium!

239. Hey Mr. Scott what you gonna do, what you gonna do, make our dreams come true!

240. Threat Level Midnight

Questions 241-260

241. Who was the trainer of Michael Scarn in Threat Level Midnight?

242. Who did Jim play in Threat Level Midnight?

243. Pam ruined which one of Jim's pranks by laughing (after moving to sales)?

244. How did Meredith get Rabies?

245. What did Michael 'Carb Load' on before the Rabies run?

246. What was Michael's response to Darryl saying, 'He's happy!' As he fed a Squirrel before the Rabies run?

247. What did Dwight give birth to when Michael was planning for Jan's baby to be born?

248. What is the name of Andy's college singing group?

249. What street do Jim and Pam live on? What's it by?

250. Why did Creed file a complaint that the bathrooms were whites only?

251. What were the two options the office could choose to buy with the year-end surplus?

252. What/where did Michael buy when he decided to give back the surplus for a bonus (he never followed through)?

253. Where did Roy leave Pam on one of their dates?

254. What was Dwight eating when he walked in to see others feasting on Brownies? (Frame Toby)

255. What is Dwight's favorite color of shirt?

256. What did Dwight say when Jim suggested they get Packer to leave with a prank saying he'd won Justin Bieber tickets?

257. What of Hollys did Michael knock into the trash and pour salad dressing on?

258. What did Michael awkwardly say to the stripper during his dance at Bob Vance's bachelor party?

259. What was the name of Angela's cat that Dwight killed?

260. What did Michael call Angela's dead cat as he spoke to everyone when they got mad at him for hitting Meredith with his car?

Answers 241-260

241. Cherokee Jack

242. Golden Face

243. Adding more keys to Dwight's key ring in hopes that his pants would fall down.

244. Dwight trapped a bat in a garbage bag over her head

245. Fettuccine Alfredo

246. He's happy because he's insane!

247. A watermelon

248. Here Comes Treble

249. Linden Ave. By the quarry.

250. The man on door sign was white

251. Chairs or a Copier

252. Fur coat from Burlington Coat Factory

253. A high school hockey game

254. Beef Jerky

255. Mustard Yellow

256. Who's Justice Beaver?

257. Woody from Toy Story

258. Do you use Tide? Tide detergent? You smell like Tide

259. Sprinkles

260. Prinkles

Questions 261-280

261. Finish the phrase: They call it Scranton, what? _____

_____ _____

262. What was the last name of the insurance salesman Michael thought was mafia?

263. What did company the 'mafia' insurance salesman work for?

264. What did Michael say the 'mafia' insurance salesman 'Vaguely threatened him with'?

265. What were the medals made of during the Office Olympics?

266. What cellular device was given to all essential employee personnel during the Dunder Mifflin Infinity launch?

267. Why did Phyllis not like using her company issued BlackBerry?

268. What position did Pam make up when her sales weren't going well?

269. What was the punch called that was served during Dwight's Christmas celebration?

270. What was Dwight doing when Pam, Kevin, and Erin showed up at his farm to stop the Doomsday Device?

271. How many strikes until the Doomsday Device would detonate?

272. What time did the email from the Doomsday Device get sent out?

273. What was the reason for Creed's 'Distinct old man smell'?

274. Where did Jim propose to Pam?

275. What was the Office Olympics event called that involved shuffling a distance on paper boxes?

276. What did Andy hide on top of the supply shelf for Dwight to find in order to return a favor?

277. What is on the sticker stuck to the filing cabinet at Dwight's desk?

278. What did Michael get Joe (Sabre CEO) as a going away present?

279. What was the prize for winning the basketball game?

280. What is the coveted award won by Dunder Mifflin employees?

Answers 261-280

261. The Electric City

262. Grotti

263. Mutual of Harrisburg

264. Testicular Cancer

265. Yogurt lids and Paper clips

266. Blackberrys

267. The buttons were to small

268. Office Administrator

269. Gluevine

270. Digging a horse grave

271. 5

272. 5 O' Clock

273. He was sprouting Mung Beans on a damp paper towel in his desk drawer. Very nutritious but smell like death.

274. Rest Stop halfway between Scranton and NYC

275. Flonkerton

276. Starbucks Gift Card

277. Froggy 101

278. A piece of coal from the Anthracite museum

279. Not having to come in on Saturday

280. Dundee

Questions 281-300

281. What was odd about Phyliss's Dundees nameplate?

282. Why did Dwight get pulled over while escorting Jim and Pam to the hospital?

283. What was used to quiet Michael and Dwight from fighting in Meredith's van on the way to the hospital?

284. What snack food was popular at the Michael Scott Paper Company?

285. Who originally wrote the quote on the white board at the Michael Scott Paper Company?

286. During the downfall of the Michael Scott Paper Company, what did Michael say he thought would be the saddest day of his life?

287. What did Michael host in order to drum up more business for the Michael Scott Paper Company?

288. What did Dwight say to intimidate Danny Cordray in the client's lobby?

289. Michael did not work for a week straight when he first discovered what?

290. What animal was in the video everyone watched instead of Michael's printer fire press conference?

291. What did Darryl have Andy do as he did a demo of Sabre printers to see if they caught fire?

292. What program did Ryan as CEO want everyone to use?

293. Why did Pam go to NYC?

294. What was name of the place Pam went to in NYC?

295. Why did Michael send Pam back to the office during Career Day?

296. What is the name of Pam's mom?

297. What is the name of the woman Dwight dates from Jim and Pam's wedding?

298. What is the name of the restaurant where Michael became 'Date Mike'?

299. What is the name of Stanley's wife?

300. What is the name of Stanley's mistress?

Answers 281-300

281. It said Bushiest Beaver instead of Busiest Beaver

282. Impersonating a police officer

283. Water in a spray bottle

284. Cheese balls

285. Wayne Gretzky -- Michael his (Gretzkys) name in quotes and put his own name as the writer

286. When Steve Martin died

287. Pancake Luncheon

288. She said, 'That's the biggest penis I've ever seen!' And I said, 'That's why I took you to the penis museum where tickets are a $1,000 dollars!'

289. YouTube

290. Baby otter

291. Talk higher and higher

292. Microsoft PowerPoint

293. Art school

294. Pratt School of Design

295. To get a new piece of paper

296. Heleen

297. Isabelle

298. Sid and Dexters

299. Terry

300. Cynthia

Questions 301-320

301. What did Michael think Jan's baby's name was?

302. What was Michael's Secret Santa gift to Ryan?

303. What did Jim get Pam for a Secret Santa gift (including color)?

304. What did Jim TAKE back from the teapot he gave Pam? When did this resurface again?

305. What is the name of Michael's realtor (first and last)? What is interesting about her in real life?

306. What celebrity appeared in the Sabre welcome video?

307. What was the minority management program through Sabre called?

308. How did Michael determine that Phyllis's friend, who Phyllis wanted to set Michael up with, was fat?

309. What was the job of the lady Pam chose to go on a blind date with Michael?

310. What rumor did Michael make up for Kevin to cover up his rumor about Stanley?

311. What rumor did Michael make up for Kelly to cover up his rumor about Stanley?

312. What rumor did Michael make up for Dwight to cover up his rumor about Stanley?

313. What rumor did Michael make up for himself to cover up his rumor about Stanley?

314. What rumor did Michael make up for Creed to cover up his rumor about Stanley?

315. What rumor did Michael make up for Oscar to cover up his rumor about Stanley?

316. What rumor did Michael make up for Toby to cover up his rumor about Stanley?

317. What kind of car does Stanley drive?

318. What does Creed do upon arriving late and Michael saying, 'There's been a murder'?

319. Who was the killer in the board game played to distract from the fact Dunder Mifflin was closing?

320. What level of suspicion did Dwight say was most important when choosing the killer? (Board game)

Answers 301-320

301. Asturd

302. A video iPod

303. A light blue teapot with memory's they had inside. A ketchup packet, Jim's yearbook photo

304. An envelope with a letter he wrote. He gave it to her in Season 9 along with a video of them over the years after she thought she (Pam) wasn't enough for him.

305. Carol Stills / She is Steve Carrel's wife

306. Christian Slater

307. The Print in All Colors Initiative

308. Michael asked if she could fit in a rowboat / could she and Jim fit comfortably in a rowboat together

309. Pam's landlord

310. That there's another person inside of him working him with controls

311. That she has an eating disorder

312. That he uses store bought manure

313. That he was a J-Crew model

314. He has Asthma

315. He was the voice of the Taco Bell dog

316. That he was a virgin

317. White Chrysler 300

318. He says he has to grab something from his car and takes off out of the parking lot

319. Beatrix Bourbon

320. The person he most medium suspects

Questions 321-340

321. What was the name of the murder mystery game played in Season 6?

322. What is the security guards full (First and last) name?

323. What is the name of Michael's improv character who has no sight?

324. What does Darryl tell Michael is a gang way to attack someone?

325. What color is the jersey that Darryl's sister was wearing when Dwight and Toby did surveillance to verify Darryl's workman's comp filing?

326. What did Michael order on his date with Pam's Blind Date choice?

327. What was the name (First and Last) of Michael's mistress?

328. What was the occupation of Michael's Mistress' husband?

329. What was the name of Michael's book he was going to write? What would the cover look like?

330. What was the last dish Pam and Kevin had before Pam went into labor?

331. What was the name of the all-day gorge fest Kevin and Pam had during her pregnancy?

332. What did Andy order from the new coffee shop Dwight put in as he walked into work?

333. What was the name of coffee shop Dwight put in Dunder Mifflin?

334. What was odd about the way Michael highlighted notes in his Rolodex?

335. Which lake did the booze cruise take place on?

336. Which lake did the Beach Games take place at?

337. Who was the only employee not allowed at the Beach Games?

338. What name did Jim keep saying to annoy Dwight? It was the name Jim chose for his team.

339. What was the first event of the Beach Games?

340. What did Jim and Pam buy at the garage sale during the Rabies awareness run?

Answers 321-340

321. Belles, Bourbon, and Bullets

322. Hank Tate

324. Fluffy Fingers

323. Blind Guy McSqueezy

325. Dark Green

326. Hot Chocolate with Peppermint

327. Donna Newton

328. Little league Baseball coach

329. Somehow, I Manage, and he would be in front shrugging with his sleeves rolled up

330. Macaroni and Cheese

331. Ultrafeast

332. Blueberry Muffin

333. Dwight's Caffeine Corner

334. Most colors mean don't say it

335. Lake Wallenpaupack

336. Lake Scranton

337. Toby

338. Voldemort

339. Egg Race

340. Lamp

Questions 341-360

341. What was the name on Andy's auto mechanic costume in the mafia episode?

342. What did Andy say was 'leaky' on the mother and childs car after the battery exploded?

343. What does the first building in the intro say?

344. What was the name of Michael's old boss?

345. How did Michael's old boss die?

346. What color was Michael's neon beer sign that Jan hated?

347. What was the name of Jan's candle company?

348. How much did Michael ask Andy and Jim to invest in Jan's candle company?

349. What term of endearment did Michael and Jan use excessively during the dinner party?

350. What was the name of David Wallace's invention?

351. What did Michael bring to the party at David Wallace's house?

352. What did Dwight do upon not finding Pam's iPod shuffle while they were on their way to the hospital?

353. What was the name of the MP3 player Roy gave Pam?

354. What are that Pam drew was hung up in the office by the front desk?

355. What was the color of the MP3 player Roy gave Pam?

356. What was unusual about the Schrute's wedding ceremony?

357. What did Mose do with the cars he parked during the Garden Party?

358. What kind of car did Andy sell to Dwight?

359. What kind of car does Andy drive? What color?

360. Why was Dwight late to meet Ryan, Michael and Pam for lunch?

Answers 341-360

341. Pat

342. Leaky Sparktube

343. Penn Paper

344. Ed Truck

345. According to Creed he was drunk as a skunk and slid his motorcycle under a semi which decapitated him

346. Blue

347. Serenity by Jan

348. $10,000

349. Babe

350. Suck It. A toy Vacuum to teach kids how to pick up after themselves.

351. Potato Salad

352. He found mold and smashed out all the cabinets. First, he read a good book and went to bed and started the next day

353. Prism DuroSport

354. Her watercolor of the Scranton Industrial Park building

355. Green

356. The bride and groom marry standing in their own graves

357. Tried to jump them with a moped. Stopped at the end of the ramp and jumped across all of them

358. Xterra

359. Silver Toyota Prius

360. He said he hit a bear

Questions 361-380

361. What was interesting about the flasher sketching Pam drew?

362. What was the name of the morbidly obese employee that transferred from Utica?

363. What was Michael and Jan's safe word?

364. What did Dwight form after Phyllis was flashed?

365. What did Dwight say was a concern if his petition for more floodlights in the parking lot was passed?

366. What did Dwight remove from the kitchen after Phyllis got flashed?

367. Where did Michael get the questions to determine if Meredith was an alcoholic?

368. What business did Michael and Dwight steal a client list from?

369. What mistake did the GPS make Michael do?

370. What was missing from the gift basket Michael gave to a former client?

371. What is the mall most frequented by employees?

372. What store did Michael tell the women on Women's Appreciation day, they could get one thing they wanted, and he'd buy it?

373. What flavor of Jello did Michael put Dwight's stapler in?

374. What character did everyone compare Kevin too in a YouTube video?

375. What surprise did Michael have for Charles Minor?

376. What would Dwight not give up when Pam had morning sickness?

377. What would Meredith not give up when Pam had morning sickness?

378. What did the Korean translate to on the Michael Scott Paper company delivery van?

379. What large retail store did Dwight work at upon leaving Dunder Mifflin?

380. What happened after Michael left Jan a voicemail breaking up with her?

Answers 361-380

361. It looked like Dwight but with a mustache

362. Anthony (Tony) Gardner

363. Foliage

365. It may cast more light on the penises

364. Anti-Flashing Task Force

366. Bananas

367. Mormon Church Website

368. Later putting them out of business. Prince Family Paper

369. Turn right, into a lake

370. Chocolate Turtles

371. The Steamtown Mall

372. Victoria's Secret

373. Lemon aka Yellow

364. Cookie Monster

375. He cut all the bagels into a 'C'

376. Hard Boiled Eggs

377. Smoking cigars

378. Alleluia Church of Scranton

379. Staples

380. Jan appeared in his office before he was done

Questions 381-400

381. What was Kelly confused about as she gave away her winter coats before she moved with her boyfriend, Ravi?

382. Instead of a baby climbing out if Andy's butt; what tattoo did Pam have the tattoo artist ink on his rear end?

383. What did Michael order to give in exchange for a hot dog when Jim left him at a gas station?

384. What did Michael do in the wet cement outside the office building?

385. What kept Jim and Pam from being able to sleep while having an overnight at Schrute Farms?

386. What did Dwight drop onto the trampoline for a test run before Michael would jump?

387. What do Kevin use as shoes after his were thrown away by the hotel?

388. What injury did Andy sustain while dancing in Niagara Falls?

389. How many episodes are in season 1?

390. How many episodes are in season 2?

391. How many episodes are in season 3?

392. How many episodes are in season 4?

393. How many episodes are in season 5?

394. How many episodes are in season 6?

395. How many episodes are in season 7

396. How many episodes are in season 8

397. How many episodes are in season 9?

398. How many seasons are there?

499. How many episodes are there all together?

400. What is Michael's full name?

Answers 381-400

381. She thought they were moving to Miami, Florida instead they were going to Miami, Ohio

382. A Nard Dog

383. His watch

384. Put his face print in it

385. Dwight was crying because Angela left him

386. Watermelon

387. Kleenex Boxes

388. Tore his scrotum

389. 6

390. 22

391. 23

392. 14

393. 28

394. 26

395. 26

396. 24

397. 23

398. 9

399. 201

400. Michael Gary Scott

401. What is Jim's full name?

402. What is the Scranton strangler's real name?

403. What is Pam's full name?

404. What is Dwight's full name?

405. What is Andy's full name?

406. What is Kelly's full name?

407. What is Ryan's full name?

408. What is Erin's full name?

409. What is Kevin's full name?

410. What is Darryl's full name?

411. What is Angela's full name?

412. What is Phyllis's full name?

413. Who played michael and jim's characters on the British version of the office? What are the characters names and who plays them in real life?

414. What is Gabe's full name?

415. What is Meredith's full name?

416. What is Stanley's full name?

417. What is Creed's full name?

418. What is Oscar's full name?

419. What is Toby's full name?

420. What is Jan's full name?

Answers 401-420

401. James Duncan Halpert

402. George Howard Skub

403. Pamela Morgan Beesly Halpert

404. Dwight Kurt Schrute III (aka Dwight Danger Schrute)

405. Andrew "Nard Dog" Baines Bernard

406. Kelly Rajnigandha Kapoor

407. Ryan Bailey Howard

408. Kelly Erin Hannon

409. Kevin Jaye Malone

410. Darryl Mathias Philbin

411. Angela Noelle Martin

412. Phyllis Dorthy Lapin Vance

423. David Brent - Ricky Gervais. Tom Canterbury - Martin Freeman

414. Gabriel Susan Lewis

415. Meredith Elizabeth Palmer

416. Stanley James Hudson

417. Creed Rowland Bratton

418. Oscar Juan Paul Martinez

419. Toby Wyatt Flenderson

420. Jan Levinson Gould

Questions 421- 440

421. What is Nellie's full name?

422. What is Robert's full name?

423. What is Roy's full name?

424. What is Pete's full name?

425. What is Clark's full name?

426. What is Deangelo's full name?

427. What is Holly's full name?

428. What is Jo's full name?

429. What is Karen's full name?

430. What is Josh's full name?

431. What is David's full name?

432. What actors share a first name with the character they play?

433. Song Michael uses to entice people into cafe disco

434. Gabe's middle name

435. What Michael sells at his telemarketing job?

436. Name of booze cruise captain

437. Name of the bad pizza place Michael orders from for Ryan's launch party? What's the good pizza place?

438. State Michael moves to with Holly

439. Specific city Michael moves to with Holly

440. Nickname of large warehouse employee played by Patrice O'Neal

Answers 421- 440

421. Eleanour Donna "Nellie" Bertram

422. Robert California

423. Royson "Roy" Allan Anderson

424. Peter Zachary "Plop" Miller

425. Clark Green (AKA Dwight Jr)

426. Deangelo Jeremitrius Vickers

427. Holly Partridge Flax

428. Joleen MaryAnn "Jo" Bennett

430. Josh Porter

429. Karen Filipeli

431. David Timothy Wallace

432. Angela, Phyllis, Clark and Creed (Creed Bratton is played by Creed Bratton)

433. Gonna make you sweat (everybody dances now)

434. Susan

435. Diet pills (lipophedrine)

436. Captain Jack

437. Bad: Pizza by alfredo. Good: Alfredo's pizza cafe

438. Colorado

439. Boulder

440. Sea monster

Questions 441- 460

441. Food that Ryan started the fire with

442. Name of Jan's candle company

443. Tagline of Michael's Dunder Mifflin Commercial

444. Name of Michael's offensive Asian character

445. Song Andy sings to impress Pam

446. Song Andy sings to impress Angela

447. Song Andy and Dwight sing to impress Erin

448. Receptionist who fills in for Pam whole she's at art school

449. Band Creed used to play in

450. Who is the only character whose first and last name on the show is their same name in real life?

451. Item of Dwight's that Jim puts in Jello

452. Item of Michael's that Jim puts in jello

453. Item of Andy's that Jim puts in jello

454. Break me off a piece of that _____

455. Gang resolution tactic that Darryl teaches Michael

456. Restaurant Michael plans to start even though he can't cook

457. Fancy mens shoe store Michael plans to start

458. Amount of pounds Jim pledges to lose for the weight loss initiative

459. Decapitated while driving drunk

460. Who Creed thinks was decapitated (YOU'RE NOT REAL MAN)

Answers 441- 460

441. Cheese pita

442. Serenity by Jan

443. Limitless paper in a paperless world

444. Ping

445. Rainbow connection

446. Take a chance on me

447. Country roads take me home

448. Ronni

449. the grass roots

450. Creed Bratton

451. Stapler

452. Mug

453. Calculator

454. Fancy feast

455. Fluffy fingers

456. Michael's cereal shack

457. Shoe lala

458. 65

459. Ed Truck

460. Dwight

Questions 461- 480

461. The certificate on Michael's wall proves that he is the proud owner of a

462. What part Native American does Michael claim to be

463. If they won the basketball game, where did Jim ask Pam to go with him?

464. What high school did Toby and Katy both attend

465. What kind of trophy does Kelly receive as a Dundie?

466. What is the name of the lawyer that Michael hires?

467. What game is the national sport of Icelandic paper companies?

468. Name one of Meredith's favorite movies?

469. What is the name of Michael's screenplay?

470. What is Michael's password to his computer?

471. What does Kelly get Oscar for Christmas?

472. What type of mp3 player did Roy get Pam for Christmas?

473. What does Michael order at Hooters?

474. Name one of the topics for conversation Jim and Ryan suggest to Dwight whole filling the truck

475. What is Michael's favorite NY pizza joint?

476. What was the name of the TV show Michael appeared on as a child?

477. What does the back of the jersey say that Michael gets from Dwight?

478. What causes Creed's distinct old man small

479. What World Series of Poker event did Kevin win?

480. Where does Jim say that Michael and Dwight can find gaydar?

Answers 461- 480

461. Quality seyko timepiece

462. 2/15ths

463. The outlet mall

464. Bishop O'Hara

465. A bowling trophy

466. James P. Albini

467. Flonkerton

468. Legally blonde

469. Threat level midnight

470. 123

471. Shower radio

472. Prism Duro-Sport

473. Chicken breast, hold the chicken

474. Ponies

475. Sbarro

476. Fundle Bundle

477. From Dwight #1

478. Mung beans

479. 2002 $2,500 no-limit deuce to Steven Draw

480. Sharper image

Questions 481- 500

481. What outlet store does Dwight suggest Jan go while he comes to meet her

482. What food does Michael ask for at the Diwali

483. What was Martin's crime that sent him to jail?

484. What is the name of Pam and Karen's new party planning committee?

485. What is the name of the file of Jan's racy vacation photo?

486. What is the name of Michael's computer?

487. What movie did Dwight expect to see when watching wedding crashers?

488. What does Creed say Roy attacked Jim with?

489. What actress plays Michael Scarn's wife?

490. What play was Dwight in in 7th grade? What character did he play?

491. During the screenplay reading of Threat Level Midnight who is Michael's old partner

492. What drink does Michael order at the business meeting that takes place at Chilis

493. What was the original name of Samuel L. Chang in Threat Level Midnight? How did Michael fail to change it in his script?

494. She wanted kids and her husband didn't and neither of them changed their minds

495. What does Jim make for Pam when they sit on the roof?

496. What road was Michael "born and raised on"?

497. What county is Scranton in?

498. What does Dwight call his workout ball?

499. What is the name of Jim's roommate?

500. What brand of shoes does Dwight wear to Jim's party?

Answers 481- 500

481. Liz Claiborne

482. Smores

483. Insider trading

484. The committee to plan parties

485. Jamaican Jan sun princess

486. Harvey

487. Grizzly man

489. Catherine Zeta Jones

488. A sock filled with nickels

490. 1) Oklahoma. 2) Mutie the mailman

491. Samuel L. Chang

492. Awesome blossom

493. 1) Dwight. 2) Dwigt

494. What is the reason Jan got a divorce

495. Grilled cheese sandwiches

496. Kenneth Road

497. Lackawanna County

498. A fitness orb

499. Mark

500. Birkenstocks

The Office Fun Facts

1. Michael Schur, who was a writer and producer of the show, played Dwight's cousin, Mose.

2. The casting team originally wanted John Krasinski to audition for the role of Dwight, and he ended up convincing them he would be better off as Jim Halpert.

3. When Krasinski auditioned, he accidentally told the executive producer that he was worried they were going to mess up the show since he liked the British version so much.

4. Phyllis Smith was originally only an assistant casting director for the show. But when she delivered lines to the actors auditioning, producers were so impressed that they ended up making the role of Phyllis Lapin for her.

5. Krasinski did a lot of research on Scranton and paper companies after getting the role of Jim. He shot footage of Scranton that ended up appearing in the opening credits of the show.

6. One of Michael Scott's girlfriends, Carol (the realtor), is Steve Carell's wife in real life.

7. Krasinski, Mindy Kaling (Kelly Kapoor) and Angela Kinsey (Angela Martin) were all, at one point, interns at Late Night With Conan O'Brien.

8. Jenna Fischer (Pam Beesly) kept the engagement ring that Jim gave Pam. She admitted on Twitter that it's just a silver ring that isn't worth anything, but she has held onto it anyway.

9. Fischer had been a struggling actor for eight years before getting cast on the show.

10. When the cast sang "Seasons of Love" for Michael in Season 7 (episode 21) all the actors actually cried.

Related: Jim Halpert's Funniest Quotes

11. Fischer and Kinsey are best friends in real life, even years after the show has ended. Fischer is actually the godmother to Kinsey's child. The two recently launched their own podcast together: Office Ladies.

12. During her first day on set, Rashida Jones (Karen Filippelli) laughed at Carell's improvising so much that she thought she was going to be fired.

13. The cast picked the opening theme music. U.S. series creator Greg Daniels gave them four versions of the song and told them to vote for the winner.

14. On several episodes, a Homer Simpson doll can be seen on the set. Daniels was a writer on The Simpsons, so he put the doll on the set as a nod to his past.

15. The computers on set really worked and even had the internet to make things seem more realistic. However, in the first season, everyone's computers were fake except for the five main cast members. They didn't get WiFi until 2006.

16. Carell almost didn't get to play Michael Scott because he was committed to another NBC show called Come to Papa. When that didn't work out, he was able to commit to The Office.

17. Still, it wasn't until after his role in 2005's the 40-Year-Old Virgin that Carell became a real star and someone who got viewers excited about the show.

18. Brian Baumgartner, the actor who played Kevin Malone, went to the same high school as Ed Helms, who played Andy Bernard.

19. B.J. Novak (Ryan Howard) and Krasinski also went to the same high school.

20. The first season of the show was the one that was mostly based on the British version of The Office. Critics hated it and no one felt optimistic about the show's future. Producers responded by making Michael more optimistic and likable.

21. Seth Rogen, Patton Oswalt, Judah Friedlander and Matt Besser all auditioned for the role of Dwight Schrute. Meanwhile, Rainn Wilson (who actually played Dwight) had auditioned for the role of Michael.

22. Other actors who auditioned for the role of Michael included Paul Giamatti, Bob Odenkirk, Martin Short, Hank Azaria, Paul F. Tompkins, and Alan Tudyk.

23. The episode when Jim proposed to Pam included the most expensive shot ever at $250,000. The crew had to build a replica of a gas station and rest stop for the proposal scene, since filming it at an actual gas station would have cost $100,000.

24. Paul Lieberstein, who played Toby Flenderson, was a writer, producer, and director for the show, and eventually became a showrunner.

25. Kinsey and Lieberstein were in-laws in real-life—Kinsey was once married to his brother.

26. When the Stamford branch and Scranton branch merged together, the producers were originally going to get rid of all of the

Stamford characters. They ended up liking Helms so much that they made him into a series regular.

27. During one of Michael's last scenes, Pam ran up to him at the airport to say goodbye and he whispered something in her ear that viewers couldn't hear. Fischer has never revealed what he said but has said the sentiment was real.

28. Carell never watched the British version of The Office because he didn't want to subconsciously imitate Ricky Gervais'version of Michael Scott.

29. James Spader (Robert California) was only supposed to be making a cameo as a replacement for Michael, but producers liked him so much that they kept him on.

30. There was almost a spin-off to the show called The Farm starring Dwight, but it never ended up working out.

Related: The Office Reboot—Everything We Know

31. Carell sweats really easily, so the set of The Office had to be kept at 64 degrees so that his sweating wouldn't ruin the shots.

32. The episode "Beach Games" was a disaster. It was very hot during the day and then very cold at night. Everyone ate so many hot dogs that they got sick, and Wilson accidentally got sand in Leslie David Baker's eye (Stanley Hudson), and he had to go to the hospital for a scratched cornea.

33. During most of Season 3, Krasinski had to wear a wig because he had to cut his hair for the movie Leatherheads.

34. In the episode "Lecture Circuit," Dwight made a banner that said, "It is your birthday" for a birthday party. Krasinski and Wilson found it so funny that production had to shut down until they could stop laughing.

35. In the episode "Gay Witch Hunt," Carell improvised his kiss with Oscar Nunez (Oscar Martinez). When Nunez reached out for a

kiss on the cheek, Carell kissed him on the mouth unexpectedly, making his surprising reaction a legitimate one.

36. In Season 4, Kinsey was pregnant in real life and hid her stomach behind props like bags, printers, and boxes.

37. Then, in Season 8, Fischer was really pregnant and ended up coinciding with Pam's pregnancy.

38. Amy Poehler almost played the role of Jan Levinson but didn't end up getting it. She did end up starring in Parks and Recreation, which was originally a sort of spinoff of The Office.

39. Kaling and Novak were originally hired as writers for the show before getting roles. Novak was the first actor hired.

40. Amy Ryan, who played Holly Flax, got the role because the producers loved The Wire so much.

41. The show was almost called The American Workplace instead of The Office.

42. Famous directors including J.J. Abrams, Harold Ramis, Jason Reitman, Jon Favreau, and Joss Whedon have all directed various episodes of the show.

43. No one but the showrunners knew that Carell would appear in the series finale. They even kept it a secret from network executives until the show aired.

44. Mose was inspired by a character named Mose from a reality show called Amish in the City.

45. Novak actually worked with Ashton Kutcher on MTV's Punk'd in 2003 before getting hired.

46. Creed Bratton's name is actually Creed Bratton in real life.

47. Baumgartner auditioned for the role of Stanley before getting the role of Kevin.

48. Krasinski and Wilson often gave each other lines and advice while shooting scenes together.

49. When Fischer was cast as Pam, the first question she asked was if Krasinski was hired for Jim, because she could only picture him as Jim.

50. Schrute Farms has a real page on TripAdvisor with thousands of reviews…but Schrute Farms isn't a real place. The page even has a warning that says, "This is a fictional place, as seen on NBC's The Office. Please do not try to book a visit here."

51. The Dundies were based on an awards presentation that Greg Daniels did for his real-life employees on King of the Hill called the Swampies.

52. The character Jim Halpert was named after Daniels' actual friend, Jim Halpert.

Printed in Great Britain
by Amazon